I'm Not My Fault

by Don Haury

Revised Edition

Safe Place Publishing
P.O. Box 4411
Scottsdale, AZ 85261

First Published May, 1988

Expanded & Revised August, 1990

Library of Congress Catalogue Card No.: 90-091961

ISBN 0-9626323-0-9

Cover design by: Lee Beaman

Illustration by: Scott Haury

To contact the author, write to:
Don Haury
Safe Place Publishing
P.O. Box 4411
Scottsdale, Arizona 85261   Printed in the U.S.A.

To my Brothers and Sisters . . .

This book is dedicated to "you",
the most important and spectacular
creation of all time.

I'm Not My Fault

Table of Contents

Chapter 1

Prologue: The Shame-Based Co-Dependent

*"It's arrogant of me to think that I am
less than I really am"*

I am a co-dependent. This means that I am dependent on conditions outside of me to tell me who I am, what I think, and how I feel. My co-dependency is the result of my being shame-based, which means that I am missing a basic sense of value, self-worth, self esteem and importance. In essence, I feel flawed and defective. Consequently, I do not believe that I deserve good things or success.

In general, I think I am not good enough. When in doubt, I am wrong or it's my fault. And, regardless of the circumstances, I don't believe that I have much to contribute. I have such a tremendous fear of being judged or criticized that I desperately try to hide for fear that someone will expose what I know about myself.

Regarding relationships, I can't imagine that a woman would like me just because of who I am. Nor can I imagine that someone would want to spend time with me, just because I'm me, without an ulterior motive. Oh sure, if I had a big job or lots of money, or a big boat or expensive car, then I could understand. But not just because someone simply enjoys being with me.

1

Some people might have a healthy positive identity, others might even have a somewhat neutral identity that says "I really don't know about me." But not me. Mine is the identity of a shame-based person, a "worth-less" self perception that is almost entirely negative. I simply do not have the ability to believe that I have any healthy attributes, and don't seem to be able to generate a satisfactory relationship with myself. I criticize myself unmercifully, as though I'm bound and determined to change my unacceptable self.

Everything and everybody seems more important than I am. I just don't matter much in this world. Most everyone else is more capable than I am, better than I am, and deserves more than I do. I try to tell myself that it's not true, that I am OK and capable and worthy, but a strong voice in my mind overrides me and says that's not true. I feel that I am missing whatever it is that is supposed to make life work. My co-dependent behavior is the result of this overall negative self concept, my feeling "a-shamed" about who I am.

Shame can be defined as feeling exposed or naked. When I have what is called a "shame attack," I feel that my inadequacy and defectiveness have been exposed. If someone sees my truth, they see me as the failure that I feel I am and I sink into a depressive "what's the use" condition. Most of my decisions and actions in life have been an attempt to hide this reality from myself and everyone else.

I'm Not My Fault

Somehow, I have always believed that what I've done and who I became was my fault, as if I made me this way. This is not true, but I didn't realize this fact until I started my recovery from shame-based co-dependency.

What happens when I have this defective self-concept (or shame-based condition)? I walk around the planet feeling badly about myself and who I am, and my prevailing attitude is one of "struggling to be OK" just to survive. I have even contemplated suicide. After all, I don't matter much and no one would care. My life is a series of problems to solve rather than an enjoyable experience.

I probably wouldn't be here today, except that the strongest natural instinct for human beings is survival. It seems that whether I like it or not, I have had an inherent desire to persist. So, my dilemma has been that the truth about me was intolerable, yet I somehow needed to go on.

Fortunately for me, I found alcohol along the way to ease some of the pain and quiet the fears. It allowed me to feel alive for the first time. What I didn't realize was that my need to use alcohol for relief from my shame would inevitably lead to alcoholism, with all of the debilitating consequences. The pain of this solution eventually became too great, forcing me to give it up.

Since childhood I sensed that, "if someone else could tell me I'm OK, then maybe I could believe it. Just maybe, if

I could convince or prove to someone else that I'm important and worthwhile, then maybe I could believe it."

Acting on this reasoning, I entered into my disease of co-dependency. I abandoned myself in an effort to circumvent the negative feelings of shame I had about me and who I was. And, since I had learned from the beginning that I had to abandon my reality to get my needs met and feel part of, I didn't realize that I was giving up anything important.

I set out on a co-dependent course which demanded that I live from the outside in vs. the inside out. In other words, I learned to react to what was going on around me based on my quest for acknowledgement, approval or acceptance. Conversely, a healthy person lives life from the inside out, acting on or responding to outside situations based on their inner beliefs and convictions.

I abandoned myself and in doing so cut myself off from the internal voice which intuitively knew what was best for me. I had begun the search for false gods.

From then on, everything that happened outside of me determined how I felt. And that was OK with me. Anything to cover up my inner feelings. I people-pleased, putting other people and things before me. I became vulnerable to anything that could make me feel better about me, hoping beyond hope that someone would recognize me, accept me, tell me I'm worthy and important. I didn't realize that no matter how much approval or acceptance I received from others, enough would never be enough until I was truly able to accept my own reality.

I had entered the world of prostitution.

What others thought about me became paramount. I manipulated, controlled, lied, and sacrificed and compromised me, anything to improve my outside image and be recognized as a worthy, capable person. My image became who I was and I created fantasies and illusions about myself and my relationship to others. I became obsessed with anything that would help to perpetuate my lie — alcohol, drugs, food, sex, gambling or work. I created illusion after illusion in an effort to produce a satisfactory image that would allow me to continue to escape.

But all the while I knew, deep down inside, that I was a fraud. Some shame-based people I have known seem to be able to block out their truth altogether and continue to live as images. They have mastered the art of focusing completely on others instead of themselves, blaming people and conditions for their feelings and everything that's wrong. At times I've tried that too.

Sooner or later, I had to fail in my desperate attempt to control and perpetuate my false image, my lie. When I finally lost control, I reached despair. The hopelessness I felt at this point became the opportunity for my recovery. But I didn't recognize it at the time.

My recovery from co-dependency and any other addictive or compulsive behavior is my recovery from shame.

I will make a statement which will aid your recovery if you will allow yourself to believe it — "Who you are and what you've become is not your fault." As a matter of fact, I'll go on to say that you had no choice but to become who you are and to do what you've done — it couldn't have been any different.

I hope you can feel a little sadness or pain, or get a little angry about that fact.

The following will show you how you became shame-based and inherited your co-dependent behavior. I hope it will help you to join me in saying " I'm not my fault."

Chapter 2

Understanding the "Why" of Shame & Co-Dependency

"It would be egotistical of me to think
that I created my own demise."

When I was born I was instinctively aware of the need for survival, the strongest drive in each of us. I sensed a need to be taken care of, a need for someone to feed and shelter me if I was going to make it. This need made me totally vulnerable to my original caretakers, mom and dad. Without them, I would die. For this reason, the fear of abandonment is the most intense primary fear of every child.

I assumed that mom and dad were gods. After all, isn't a god a supreme being who is the creator and ruler of my universe? This sure defined mom and dad.

I had no idea that I was really a child of a Divine Creator who simply used my mom and dad as vehicles to get me here. Their duty was to honor my preciousness, to nurture, love, teach and support me. In reality my bed should have been like a manger, and I was entitled to three wise men. And, I deserved gold, frankincense and myrrh, too.

Instead, it was "just give that kid a bottle every couple of hours and hope to hell he doesn't cry all night and keep us awake. Cute though, isn't he, for a boy. Oh God, I

7

didn't realize he'd be this much trouble, and that smell is just awful."

"Audacity" is the word that comes to mind when I think about it. Mom and dad not only inferred that they were gods, but assured me it was true. They said I belonged to them, that I was their kid. They felt that they had the right to raise me to be whatever they wanted me to be. And I believed them. After all, I had no second opinion or other logic on which to base another conclusion. So I became theirs and they were my gods.

Henceforth came the gospel according to mom and dad. Their rules and regulations became my commandments. How they acted in my presence and how they treated me became synonymous with who and what I was. If they treated me as though I was bad, I was a bad person. If they didn't pay attention to me, I wasn't worthy of attention. If they noticed only the things I did that they thought were wrong, I was inadequate and incapable. If I sensed being in the way, I was not important. If they looked at me in disgust, I was disgusting. If they ignored me, I was nobody. The list goes on and on.

I believe that these perceptions are the core from which all of my false beliefs about who I think I am were born. Rather than creating an environment where my special gifts and talents could be nurtured, supported and expressed, my parents were only interested in molding me into what they wanted me to be. No wonder I arrived in adulthood without any sense of identity. It had been constantly denied, criticized and covered up.

It's important to note how my parent's actions and messages reflected shame as opposed to guilt. Guilt is about something we did, whereas shame is about who we are. The assumption of shame came from their actions and the responses I received when I made errors or broke rules. Mom and dad's responses reflected that there was something wrong with my very being, rather than what I did. If I didn't do something in accordance with their beliefs, the feedback was "what did you do that for, stupid?", "you're wrong", or "you're a bad boy." This didn't let me know that I was OK, that I'd simply made a mistake and done something they thought was wrong. It told me that I am stupid, that something is wrong with me, and that I am bad.

The following questions relate to how we were treated. I hope they will open the door to awareness about your shame and how you got it.

Answering yes or no, on a somewhat continuing basis did your mom, dad, and/or a significant other:

- support the fact that you were a precious, worthwhile person, when you weren't doing anything?

- respect and support your ideas, beliefs, feelings and space?
- spend time with you in an effort to teach and understand you?
- exhibit that they enjoyed being with you?
- take an interest in what you were interested in?
- go out of their way to help you, without your asking?
- support your just being human when you made mistakes?
- stay with you while you were hurting, acknowledging that it's OK to hurt?
- confirm that you are OK, right where you are?
- accept you for just being you?
- spend time with you when you were frustrated, angry, sad, or depressed, and not tell you what you should do or how you should change or feel?
- support the fact that it's OK for you to do whatever you need to do to take care of yourself, first?

"Yes" answers to these questions indicate the active presence of love, which produces a healthy sense of self and self-worth. If you have honestly answered yes to most questions, you probably have a good self-concept, unless you are still in denial as the result of your fantasy bonding. "Fantasy bonding" becomes our conscious reality when we've created and believed happy illusions about our childhood to protect ourselves and our families from the pain of the abusive truth. It was necessary to survive, so we couldn't let ourselves see a painful truth about someone we desperately needed. This bonding will persist even today if we "need" our parents support in any way, or if we are still protecting them.

"No" answers show neglect and emotional abandonment, which initiates the shame-based condition. If love has an opposite, it would be shame, since loves adds value to, and shame takes value from. Shame is about feeling like a failure as a person, that we have failed at being what we were supposed to be. We become ashamed of who we are, what we know (or don't know), and what we do.

To see how shame may have been further magnified in your life, answer the following slightly altered questions:

On a somewhat continuing basis, did your mom, dad and/or a significant other —

- support the fact that you were not worthy if you weren't doing something
- discount your ideas, beliefs, feelings and boundaries?
- exhibit that you were bothering them with your questions and your desire to understand?

- act like you were in the way?
- put down things you were interested in?
- chide you about your needing help, or offer to help only begrudgingly and on their terms?
- leave you while you were hurting, saying that it'll be OK?
- say or imply that you'll never make it being who you are?
- tell you or suggest that you should be like someone else?
- say to you when you were frustrated, angry, sad or depressed that you shouldn't feel the way you do, then tell you how you should feel?
- express the fact that it's not OK for you to do whatever it is you need to do to take care of yourself?
- make it clear to you that it's their way or no way (or the highway), that your way of thinking was wrong?
- make fun of and ridicule you?
- defy you to get angry or talk back to them?

Remembering that how you were treated determined how you feel about yourself, you might start seeing why you have negative ideas about who you are and what you're capable of. These are the messages that cause our feelings of fear, emptiness, being different, less than, alone and not belonging, even when we are with others. I suggest that you answer the questions again for each significant person you have had in your life. Then you will better understand specifically who the culprits were or are.

These messages put my very being under attack, rather than giving me constructive criticism about what I had done. The messages did not reflect that I was a worthwhile human being and child of a Divine Creator. As a matter of fact, they denied that possibility altogether.

Similar put downs, or shaming, took place regarding my feelings. I can't tell you how many times I've heard "You shouldn't feel that way — what's the matter with you?" or "You hurt your mother's feelings — you should know better than that," or "Oh come on, that wasn't a big deal." Over and over again, the words were about my very personhood, that I shouldn't feel the way I did, that my feelings didn't count or were wrong, or that I was responsible for how others felt, and their feelings were more important than mine.

This conditioning told me that everyone else is more important than I am, and that I am acceptable only when I put everyone else before me.

I didn't know that feelings are not good or bad, that they just are, and they are who I am. For many of us, it is difficult to identify how shame was perpetrated in our families, because most of the messages that shamed us are so common place in our society.

A common family and societal dysfunction is the "Blame and Shame Game." Many people blame others or conditions for what they do or what happens to them, and shame-based people often let them get away with it. Many times I have fallen prey to comments like "see what you made me do," "this is your fault," "if only you ...," "you caused me to...," "if it hadn't been for you, I ...," or "you hurt my feelings." Today I realize that these types of statements are made by people who are not willing to accept responsibility for their own feelings and actions, and choose instead to play the victim game by scapegoating me.

The following is another example of how I was shamed. As a child, I shut the door on my finger. I went to tell mom that my finger was hurt. She looked at it, kissed it and said "It's OK, now go out and play." I went out to play, but my finger still hurt. But mom said that it was OK now. So I figured that something must be wrong with me, because it shouldn't hurt.

To ignore my pain and invalidate the reality of my feelings is to discount my very existence. And remember, I was hearing this from my gods, therefore it was absolute truth.

Because I believed these truths, the following unhealthy thoughts became my permanent reality:

- I am always expected to know or know better.
- I never feel welcomed or that I belong unless someone else says it's OK.
- I feel like a failure because I can't do what everyone else can do. I "S"hould "H"ave "A"lready "M"astered "E"verything.
- How dare I fail to be there for someone else, after all they did for me.
- Who am I to think I have the right to ask you to support or help me?
- I shouldn't be afraid.
- I can't do (or say) that — it might hurt their feelings, and their feelings are more important than mine.
- How dare I think that I know (what's right, the way, what's good for us or me) — I don't know what I'm talking about.
- It's not Ok for me to enjoy myself.
- I should never put me or my interests first.
- How dare I take care of me — without considering you.
- I'm afraid I will look like a fool if I express my needs or wants.
- It's not OK to say "no", especially without a very good reason.
- I should be grateful for the little I get,because I really

don't deserve much.

- It's not OK to play or enjoy myself, unless I've taken care of everything I "should" do first.
- If I don't do it your way, you will abandon me.
- If I stand up for me, to you, something bad will happen.
- If I quit, I'm a failure.

Who we are is confirmed by how others treat us, and this validation becomes our self-concept, subject to further confirmation. This self-concept then becomes the basis from which we make all of our choices in life. A negative self-concept will foster unhealthy choices. In a society full of self-righteous, shame-based people trying to hide their own shame and prove they're OK, it is not difficult to have one's negative self-concept confirmed. And when it's confirmed, it becomes our truth.

As I went off to participate in society, play, church, school and to be with friends, I was hoping that somehow my opinions about me were not true. I didn't realize that I would always gravitate toward the "familiar", which is a derivative of the word "family". So, I was naturally drawn toward people who behaved and treated me like my family did, simply because what is familiar is comfortable. How was I to know that familiar would always win over change or something different. I didn't have a clue about what was really going on — that like attracts like because of an inherent feeling of familiarity.

My family attracted other people who acted like they did and I attracted people who either felt like I did or acted like they did. Talk about a no-win deal! It was easy and natural for me to find people who would confirm that I was bad, unimportant, and not good enough, which confirmed my "shame-based" condition. This confirmation, coming from outside of my family, assured me that the messages I had received from them were correct. I believe that most of us have experienced a particular incident or event with someone outside our family, yet "familiar", that locked in and confirmed that we should be a-shamed of who we are.

I didn't realize that my parents and friends were living with the same condition I was, which they were also desperately trying to hide. They didn't know what was going on either. Since they couldn't tell anyone about their shame and who they really feared they were, they put together a "this-is-who-I-am" act which became their identity. They presented it to the world, hoped it would be an acceptable "image" and continually adjusted it to suit the circumstances. By the time I came along, their "image reality" was the only reality they knew. They were living in a world of illusions and images, with a "make-believe" identity, determined to make it real.

Finally, as parents, they were authorities. "Opinion-
ated self-righteousness" became the norm, and we got killed.
Although they were sometimes compliant on the streets they
were Hitlers at home. As their kids, we had to live up to their
purported identity. That is why I feel like I was raised as an
image, by two images. I had no other choice except to put an
act together just like they had. No wonder I struggle today,
trying to figure out who I really am.

And the process goes on, generation after generation.

During my recovery in a Twelve-Step program, I
found myself face-to-face with my shame-based condition. I
remember my first thoughts when learning of the Fourth
Step, which says, "We made a searching and fearless moral
inventory of ourselves," followed by the Fifth Step which
says, "We admitted to God, to ourselves, and to another
human being, the exact nature of our wrongs." "Oh no", I
thought, "now they want me to expose my inadequacy and
worthlessness to myself, God and the world. Now they want
me to expose the truth that I've been desperately trying to
hide from myself and everyone else, my entire life." My
thought was, "No way!" Looking back, I realize that I felt like
they were asking me to admit my shame. The problem was,
it was my only reality at the time.

Another example comes from a meeting where the
topic was the Fourth Step. A person new to the program

commented that she thought she would try to work on the Fourth Step. She explained that she was afraid to tell anyone that when she looked inside to explore her inventory, she couldn't find anything or anybody. How frightening to tell someone nobody was home inside, that everything about us was phoney!

As people a-shamed of who we are, our entire existence is based on protecting and supporting a "make-believe" identity. We make dreams, fantasies and illusions our reality and we use any means to keep them alive. We use people, places or things to keep our illusions alive, trying to escape from our deeply painful feelings.

If you, like me, learned in your childhood that nothing you think or do is acceptable or OK, you have probably looked around desperately to find out what works for other people, hoping to mimic their behavior. We endlessly search outside of ourselves in an attempt to find solutions to our awful feeling reality. We are always willing to compromise or abandon ourselves for the sake of something or someone else that might help or work.

Therefore, I found myself with few convictions. I am generally willing to give up mine for your sake, or their sake, or whatever sake, in an effort to be accepted, acknowledged, belong or feel secure. Remember, no one supported or encouraged me to develop healthy boundaries or convictions for myself. As a matter of fact, they demanded that I abandon mine for theirs if I wanted to feel part of or cared for. I relate all too well to the comment "If you don't stand for something, you'll fall for anything." Even today, when I stand for what I believe in, I get the feeling that I'm going to be abandoned and/or something painful is going to happen.

I was either blindly compliant or in unwarranted conflict with others, fighting for something without knowing what it was. I now know that my fight came out of my need for self respect and an identity, which I didn't know how to achieve. I've learned that self-respect is an earned commodity based on standing up for one's own value system.

I could not establish any healthy values because I was attempting to get my needs met in a family which expressed "conditional love", which really has nothing to do with love. It's bargaining, and mom and dad held all the cards. I had to play, my needs intuitively told me that, but it was always by their rules, whether I liked it or not. Self-compromise and self-abandonment were inevitable.

My parents, without the capacity to supply my "needs", supplied my "wants" which they interpreted as my "needs". Today, I have my wants and needs confused and constantly get them mixed up.

In an effort to understand how you have compromised or abandoned yourself, answer the following questions:

For the sake of —
- being or feeling accepted
- feeling part of (belonging)
- feeling cared about or loved
- feeling secure
- feeling free
- feeling worthy
- having fun
- companionship
- being liked
- feeling approval
- material security
- trusting or being trusted
- emotional security
- deserving pleasure
- having intimacy

I had to_____

     (or)

I had to be_____

The level of my self esteem is inversely proportional to how much I compromise whatever is in my own best interests. The more I compromise, the lower my self esteem is. So, if I had to give up my human rights "for the sake of" getting my basic needs met, I could not gain self respect or esteem. Your answers to the previous questions will show you the areas where you compromised yourself, preventing healthy growth, self respect and self esteem.

Fill in the blanks again regarding your current needs, asking yourself, "For the sake of, I have to _____ (or) I have to be _____. " This will help you to recognize areas where you continue to compromise (or sell out) yourself.

My shame-based condition causes me to feel that I am inadequate and incapable. This "truth" seriously questions my ability to survive on my own and makes me very insecure. My internal voice says "If I am left alone with only my own devices, without any help, I won't make it." I will not be able to take care of myself, by myself.

The resultant feelings of fear are overwhelming. I then sense a need to link up with someone who will help me to survive. I become extremely vulnerable to anyone or any condition that I think might help me to make it. In this vulnerable frame of mind, I run a huge risk of falling prey to someone who is seeking power over another human being. These people look strong on the outside, but are in reality as shame-based as I am, keeping their fears hidden under an egocentric mask and looking for a "hostage" to help them feel more secure.

A common denominator for shame-based co-dependents is that either nobody is home, or if someone is, they are "not good enough". We respond in either of two ways. If we have not developed a strong alter-ego, we become "compliant subordinates" and frequently find ourselves in a victim role. On the other hand, the "arrogant know-it-alls" who have strong alter-egos become the victimizers. Most of us bounce back and forth between the two, our shame reality and our image reality, feeling less than or better than, but rarely equal to, those around us. It's interesting to note that although these external personalities are opposite, the fear ridden shame-based condition is the same.

There is hope for change and recovery.

It begins when we start to believe that we are precious worthwhile human beings, not because of what we do or know, but just because we are. We are human "beings", not human "doings", and we don't need to compromise ourselves. We are entitled to be loved unconditionally, as deemed by our Creator.

The shaming which we've suffered is the cause of our dysfunction, and it has invalidated our human preciousness.

Love is its opposite and it validates wholeness and human perfection. It confirms that we are special creations of our Creator, made in His/Her image and likeness. Love tells us that we are deserving of perpetual joy, inner peace and oneness, just the way we are, without doing anything to deserve it.

Love is not just a word. It is an action which honors and validates the preciousness of another without any expectations attached to what they do or know.

If in reading this you've determined that you're involved with people who do not respect your preciousness and Divine likeness, be aware that you are permitting abuse. You are being used to satisfy other's distorted needs, and to help them hide from their truth. This new awareness can be your first on a path to a better life.

We have been taught to be subordinate, that everyone else counts more than we do and should therefore be considered before us. The summation of the messages I heard is — "How dare I put me first!" When I do, I feel very selfish, and fear subsequent abandonment and/or pain. Our goal in recovery is to change this message, to understand and believe in our preciousness and individual rights. We have the right to stand up for what's best for us, first and always. Happiness is our Creator's will for all of us.

Chapter 3

Tools for Recovery

Following are some suggestions which I hope will help you on your journey.

❏ Get selfish, understanding that it may feel strange and that you are simply doing what you need to do to take care of yourself. That's OK. I can't truly be there for anyone else unless I'm taking care of myself first. The following question has helped me to remember this principal — "Wouldn't anyone expect me to do whatever I need to do to take care of myself?" Healthy, caring people would.

❏ Honor your ability to make the right choices for yourself. An intuitive voice will always tell you what is right for you. Listen to it. Understand that "No." is a complete sentence, and that you have the right to say no without explaining or feeling guilty.

❏ Understand that what you think and feel counts. I constantly refer to the following:
It's OK for me to —
- Feel what I feel
- Want what I want
- Know what I know

- Think what I think
- Imagine what I imagine
- See and hear what I see and hear

❏ Please know that you have the following human rights:
- To decide and discern for yourself, based on what's best for you.
- To have your opinions and feelings respected.
- To feel like a capable adult.
- To feel and express anger. Anger is a healthy defense mechanism intended to protect you from danger.
- To change your mind.
- To make a "mis-take."
- To have worth and importance.
- To have fun.
- To be loved.
- To belong.
- To be free.

❏ Understand that feelings of guilt are only applicable when you violate "your" value system. As co-dependents, we often feel guilty when we fail to comply with other's so-called rules, regulations and value systems. Our recovery means learning to be attentive and true to our own values, while simply respecting the rights of others.

Learn to quietly get away from people who have all the answers and freely give advice, who blame, criticize and judge, who exude self righteousness and won't admit to making mistakes. They see you as an "object", not a valuable human being, and although they may say otherwise, they offer you no consideration regarding your best interests, highest good or a rational concept of what would be fair. In any interactions with them, the best you're ever going to do is break even.

❑ Disregard all comments involving "you should", "you better", "you ought to", and any other unsolicited advice. In my Safe Group, I make the following statement: "I ask (demand) that you honor who I am, validating that I am a precious, worthwhile child of God, no matter what I say, know or do. And I ask (demand) that you not criticize, judge or give me advice unless I ask."

❑ Realize that although we were "victims" in our childhood, we have been "volunteers" in adulthood. Anytime I'm blaming someone or something for what I do or what's happening to me, I'm not being accountable for my part. My recovery requires me to look at why I volunteered for the victim role.

❏ Know that it's OK to question everything, both past and present. Feel free to identify and explore the messages and rules that "they" gave you as being truth. I've come to recognize that most of the rules, beliefs and messages from my parents, religion, school and society were and still are focused on suppression and control, instead of honoring my gifts and acknowledging the special creation that I am.

Concerning school, an associate defined a "diploma" as a piece of paper, given by one institution to tell another institution that the recipient is controllable. It makes sense to me.

I define most religions as man's manipulation of spirituality in an effort to control and suppress mankind. What better means to use than the "fear of God." I've come to know that my Creator, or whatever you choose to call it, is pure unconditional love without criticism, judgement or any sense of negative input that would support my fear of God.

❏ Explore your concept of what you think and how you feel about a higher power, god or creator. Look back at how you acquired it and who taught it to you. Note how your concept of a god might be similar to your relationship with your parental gods. I have felt that I was supposed to be there for

God, instead of God being there for me, because that's how it was with my parental Gods. I now realize that my Creator is there for me, whether or not I'm there for It, as a functional parent would be.

❑ Feel free to disregard any concept or ideal that produces control, suppression or fear for you – or any other feeling that doesn't pertain to care, concern and unconditional love. Feel free to choose a new concept and a new set of beliefs that work for you. You have that right.

❑ Note that we live in a shame-based society, where dysfunction is the rule and the norm, rather than the exception. Therefore, few will honor your preciousness, best interests or highest good. Most people, and I include myself, are so preoccupied with trying either to prove or protect, they have little time for anything else. Also realize that we have a tendency to attract and associate with "familiar" people, meaning that we're likely to choose people who are similar to those of our "family," who will treat us like they did. With dysfunction so prevalent, I've reversed my shame-based self talk by saying to myself, "when in doubt, I'm right (or good)," or something else that is a validating and supporting message to me.

❏ If you question whether or not you were mistreated or abused, I ask you to be aware of the voices in your mind that spontaneously speak to you, and ask yourself if they criticize, judge or pick on you – and if they are with you or seem to be against you. Where did we learn this negative self talk? We didn't dream it up. The attitude that we have about ourselves can only be learned from one source, the "gods" that parented us. So, how your voices treat you is exactly how you were treated. We mimic what was modeled to us. It can't be any other way.

❏ Due to the basic absence of mature love in our lives, most of us are shame-based to some degree, immature, insecure and fearful. The self honesty that allowed me to admit these truths to myself was, I believe, my first step in recovery. Believe me, I did not want to admit anything. I now realize that as long as I was kidding or denying my reality to myself, I was going nowhere and my shame was keeping me in a delusionary state, hiding from myself and others.

My recovery has been a slow process of self exposure, first to myself, then to trusted others, taking the mask off my false self and becoming real. This became easier when I realized that who I thought I was, was not me, that who I thought I was was the result of what I was told and how I was treated.

❑ I believe that spiritual and emotional maturity are synonymous and that the following are some healthy attributes to work toward, when dealing with others.

• Honoring the differences with each other.

• Not taking sides.

• Giving equal consideration to both parties, with a functional concept of "fair."

• Respecting another's position when stating my own.

• Being able to withstand an emotional gut hit without reacting or being immobilized.

• Acting in an honorable, accountable and responsible manner.

• Valuing the "highest good" of all concerned, as the primary priority.

• Delaying gratification.

• Understanding that there is no right or wrong, good or bad.

Note: Although they are goals for me, the above attributes can also be used as a yardstick to understand the type of person that I'm dealing with.

❑ Establish your boundaries. My boundaries are invisible layers of bubbles that surround me at all times. They let me interact with others while maintaining control over the way other's interaction affects me. They protect me and my space, and I control them at all times. I decide what to let in and what to keep out, by making them screen-like, or hard and impenetrable, as well as anything in between. I can remove them completely or only certain layers as I choose. When I remove them, I am most vulnerable, therefore I only remove the appropriate layers depending on the degree to which those around me have earned my trust and are non-threatening.

I normally keep my boundaries screen-like, ready to use as necessary. Should someone accuse me or accost me threateningly, I render them impenetrable saying, "This is about them, not about me." At that moment, I collect the information in a bucket which hangs outside my boundaries. I use it to collect all comments that I haven't chosen to let pass into my being. At some time later when I am by myself, I look at the data in my bucket to see if there's anything in there that pertains to my highest good. If so, I take it in. The remainder is garbage, so I throw it away.

I can make my boundaries weak or strong, depending on the safety I sense regarding what's going on around me. When I feel threatened, I make my boundaries stronger, protecting me from those who haven't chosen to honor who I am. On the other hand, I can weaken my boundaries when interacting with people who I consider safe. Different from walls, boundaries let me interact on a feeling level, protecting me as necessary. Walls are either up, protecting and isolating me, or down, leaving me vulnerable and enmeshed, whereas boundaries let me operate between these two extremes.

❏ Review your definition of "success" and where it came from. If it involves comparing yourself to others, you're in a no-win situation. Life is not about winning. Life is about living, a process that involves finding and understanding oneself and evolving to one's highest potential, which is to "in-joy."

❏ Find a "safe" support group or 12 step meeting in your area and attend regularly. 12 step meetings include Co-Dependents Anonymous (602) 277-7991, Adult Children of Alcoholics (213) 534-1815, Alanon and Alcoholics Anonymous, to name a few. Check local listings, or the National Self-Help Clearinghouse in New York (212-642-2944). If you can't find one that works for you, start your own support group. Information about starting and running your own "Safe Group" is covered in the next section of this book.

What I have talked about here is reality—what really happened in our lives. The intention is accountability and exposure of ignorance and distorted self righteousness, not blame. Having our reality discounted and being deceived resulted in our demise. Our recovery begins with the opposite. It is time to stand up for who we really are, to honor our feelings and respect our own truth.

It is time for us to honor what has been discounted, realign what has been distorted, and recognize the beauty in ourselves.

You are as your Divine Power made you in the very beginning. Your negative perceptions about yourself come from others, not from truth. Feel good about knowing that who you were told you are is not the real you. Then begin your effort to free the beautiful person who has always lived inside you.

Should you struggle in the beginning to do this for yourself, remember me and the others who need you to walk with us, because we can't make this journey alone.

Chapter 4

Safe Groups

(Families of Choice)

THE ORIGIN OF SAFE GROUPS

After attending over 3,000 self-help meetings, including AA, Alanon, ACA and CoDA, I sensed that there was still an important ingredient missing for me. I had finally realized that I was a shame based co-dependent who had reached an addictive phase of co-dependency called alcoholism.

I came to realize that being shame based fathered my co-dependency. I analogized that I was like a furnace with a pilot light that had never worked, that I couldn't come on to life by myself. Since my pilot light didn't work, my thermostat couldn't either, therefore I became dependent on others or things to turn me on or off. And, since my pilot light had never worked, I didn't realize that it should.

Having been raised in a shame bound family with no cohesive support, I never learned to believe in or trust myself. I had always felt that it was them against me or everyone for themselves. The result was a continuous behavioral cycle of needing either to prove or protect, with no sense of what it would be like to just "be".

I felt that I needed what I never had, a family with a

functional premise who would commit to the actions of mature unconditional love. Also, since my co-dependency meant that I needed others to tell me who I was, it made sense to use my co-dependent traits in an effort to heal myself. If I could set up a situation wherein others would affirm, support and believe in me, then maybe I could start to do the same, lighting my own pilot light for the first time.

I developed the Safe Group structure and format in an attempt to provide the following:

- An atmosphere in which to build trust with myself and others.
- A sense of a functional family, with cohesive support.
- Consistent messages affirming that I'm OK and enough just as I am.
- A safe setting for others and myself to share our innermost reality, risking intimacy.
- A base of unconditional love and support, necessary to foster healthy growth and maturity.
- A condition wherein the maintainence of the individual's rights and recovery are more important than the maintainence of the group.

It is my hope that the principles outlined will give you healthy guidlines for your interactions with others, even if you do not set up your own safe group.

WHY A SAFE GROUP?

We have struggled at living, not knowing why. We don't seem to know how to make our lives work for us. We continually get involved with or perpetrate unhealthy self-defeating situations and relationships. We simply don't seem to be able to promote ourselves toward our own best interests and highest good. Although many of us get along well with others, individually we have a discouraging relationship with ourselves and our Creator. Our self concept is generally not good or non-existent. We labor at being OK or enough and we find it most difficult to attain self-respect, self-esteem and self-enjoyment.

A base of mature love is the foundation from which growth occurs. Since we didn't know it was absent from our past, our growth has been thwarted, leaving us insecure and immature. This void, combined with the shaming conditions that did exist, left us with little hope and few tools with which to build a successful life.

Here we will see that how we feel about ourselves and how we think others feel about us are the result of the treatment we received and the programming inflicted on us in our childhoods. We will realize that today's fears and shame are illusions carried with us from the past. We will come to know that who we were told we were is not us, that we are and always have been, innocent, worthy, talented offsprings of our Creator.

Because of our history, we have distorted perceptions about love and trust, and their workings in a family or social environment. We want to establish a condition we've not experienced, a functional family based on unconditional love.

We all have abused children living within us. We hope to connect with them, identify what happened, and re-parent them. To re-parent ourselves in a healthy way, we will need a loving mature adult capable of the task. Otherwise, we will have kids raising kids again and simply be disillusioned about our recovery.

We believe that the conditions we have set forth for the group are functional acts of love that nurture and foster recovery. Mature self-discipline and commitment to the principles are the cornerstones.

Our walk into spiritual maturity and healthy identities involves-

- a functional concept of what is "fair".
- not taking sides.
- being able to take an emotional gut hit, without reacting or being immobilized.
- respecting the other person's position, when stating one's own.
- honoring the differences.
- acting in an honorable, accountable and responsible manner.
- valuing the "highest good" of all involved, as the primary concern.
- delaying gratification.
- a commitment to truth, at all cost.
- understanding that there is not good or bad, or right or wrong.
- actions based on "knowing".

SAFE GROUP FORMATION & OPERATION

Group Size: Four to eight people – male & female, all male, or all female.

Time: Any time that's convenient for all. We meet each Monday at 7:30 pm and we just happen to be done by about 9:30 pm. Each group will have it's own personality and therefore it's own time table.

How To Pick Members:
This can be a tough one. Know that you are choosing your brothers and/or sisters, people with whom you'd like to establish trust. I'd suggest that you only ask someone you feel connected to, or alike — someone with whom you feel you have a lot in common — someone who you feel has the same sort of problems with life that you do.

Group Format:
We generally arrive at my apartment clubhouse fifteen to thirty minutes early for a cup of coffee and some general comraderie.

At 7:30 we sit down together and distribute the preface and group purpose statement. Someone will just start by identifying themselves, then reading the beginning paragraph of the "Group Purpose Statement". When they've finished, the person on the left or right will do the same, reading the next paragraph, with the process going on until the statement is finished. It then gets quiet. Someone will start by identifying themselves by name, then talking about some issue or condition that is on their mind. Each person normally shares from 2 to 5 minutes. When they are finished, we thank them and it gets quiet again, until someone else decides to share. We normally give everyone a chance to share once before anyone will share a second time. We continue until no one has anything else they wish to say. We generally wind up in a small discussion about a prevalent issue that was brought up in the sharing. When finished, we form a circle of hugs and say a prayer together.

A member, as part of their sharing, can ask the group to discuss a particular topic or issue that interests, concerns or confuses them. The response to this request normally takes place toward the end of the meeting.

A member, can also ask for feedback from the group. The group normally responds at the time requested and only relates their own experiences.

Each group will have it's own personality, the only common denominator is that they are all non-threatening and focus on validation, support and acceptance of one another.

GROUP PURPOSE STATEMENT
(To be read at each meeting)

We have gathered together primarily to work through and
limit the negative impact of "shame" and "fear" in our lives.
We will expose these feelings as manifested in our individual
environments, exploring their origin and confronting them
as illusionary lies perpetrated in our past. We will also
explore our ego defenses, which have served us well in
survival, but don't lend themselves to functional harmony
and connectedness.

We insist that our group be "safe", that we maintain an
atmosphere in which trust can be established and main-
tained.

Since our paramount fears are of being judged and criticized,
we hope that they will be absent from our meeting. We also
insist that we not give advice and that we phrase our comments so that they only pertain to ourselves.

Because "shame" manifests feelings of inadequacy, unim-
portance and unworthiness, we shall each make a commitment to modify these negative illusions by honoring the

preciousness, perfection, worthiness, and Godlikeness in each other.

We will attempt to help each other see that the negative feelings we have about ourselves, are simply negative illusions that bear no truth.

We ask that you leave your "self criticism" outside, and not bring it into the meeting. Doing so will give you a better opportunity to see the valuable person that you are.

We have spent much of our time and effort looking for recognition, a sense of importance, and approval in an attempt to prove to others and ourselves that we are important and of value. In doing so, we've been most vulnerable to people and situations outside of us. Our purpose here, both individually and as a group, is to validate and support each other's importance and value just as we are, when we're not "doing" anything. We also support the belief that a higher power is guiding each of us toward our highest good, that each one of us knows what's right for ourselves, requiring only validation, support and acceptance of who we are to bring it into our lives. By honoring this belief with each other, it is our hope that we will ingest a new and positive truth about ourselves, replacing the negative thoughts that fear and shame have murmured throughout our lives.

We ask each other to honor our boundaries and our truth, in that we are precious, worthwhile descendants of our Creator, no matter what we say, know or do. We also ask that there be no criticism or judgement, and that we refrain from giving advice unless asked, then only share our personal experience.

TWELVE STEPS FOR A RECOVERING HUMAN BEING

1. Admitted that I am powerless over my self-defeating thoughts, feelings and behavior, and that my life has become unmanageable.

     (and/or)

   Admitted that I am powerless over my need for
   _____, and my life has become unmanageable.

     (and/or)

   Admitted that I am powerless over my need to _____,
   and my life has become unmanageable.

     (and/or)

   Admitted that I am powerless over my fear of _____,
   and my life has become unmanageable.

     (and/or)

   Admitted that I am powerless over my shame , and my life
   has become unmanageable.

2. Came to believe that a power greater than myself could remedy my predicament.

3. Made a decision to trust in the care and guidance of my higher power, as I choose to perceive it.

4. Took an honest inventory of my history and myself.

5. Admitted to myself, my higher power and a trusted other person what I had uncovered and discovered.

6. Became entirely ready to have my higher power do for me what I cannot do for my self.

7. Sincerely asked my higher power to help me.

8. Made a list of all persons who I felt had violated or harmed me and who I felt I had violated or harmed, and became willing to set it right with them all.

                (or)

Made a list all situations wherein I had violated my value system, and became willing to amend my part in all cases.

9. Took the necessary actions to honorably correct or complete all of these situations, both past and present, except when to do so would not honor the highest good of others or myself.

10. Continued to take personal inventory, promptly addressing any discord or dysfunction.

11. Continued to improve my conscious contact with my Creator, as I perceive it, asking for the knowledge of Its will for me and the power to carry that out.

12. Having had a spiritual awakening as the result of these steps, we began to enjoy our lives, while practicing these principles in all our affairs.

Complimentary Reading Material:

"Toxic Parents" by Susan Forward

"Living in the Light" by Shakti Gawain

"The Road Less Traveled" by M. Scott Peck

"Shame Faced" by Stephanie E.

"The Family" by John Bradshaw

"Healing The Shame That Binds You" by John Bradshaw

"Codependent No More" by Melody Beattie

"Beyond Codependency" by Melody Beattie

"Facing Codependence" by Pia Mellody

"You Can Have It All" by Arnold Patent

"Death, Taxes, and Other Illusions" by Arnold Patent

"You Can Heal Your Life" by Louis Hay

"Twelve & Twelve" by Alcoholics Anonymous

A special thanks to Adele K.,
Bob H., Mike B., Rod G. and my son, Scott.
Without their friendship and support,
this book would not exist.